Rain Showers

Practicing the OW Sound

Rafael Moya

Rosen
PHONICS
READERS

Rosen
Classroom

Mr. Powers loves flowers.

Mr. Powers has many flowers.
Do you like flowers?

Mr. Powers frowns.

His flowers are turning brown.

They need a rain shower!
The rain falls down.

Mr. Powers watches
the rain shower.
He listens to the sound.

"Wow! That's a strong shower," says Mr. Powers.

Mr. Powers loves rain showers.
Rain showers help flowers!

The rain falls down.
It sinks into the ground.

The flowers take in the rain.

"Drink up, flowers,"
says Mr. Powers.

Wow!
The flowers are not brown now.